Our New Baby

© Aladdin Books Ltd 2008

Designed and produced by
Aladdin Books Ltd
PO Box 53987
London SW15 2SF

First published in 2008
in Great Britain
by Franklin Watts
338 Euston Road
London NW1 3BH

Franklin Watts Australia
Level 17/207 Kent Street
Sydney NSW 2000

Franklin Watts is a division of Hachette Children's Books an Hachette Livre UK company.
www.hachettelivre.co.uk

ISBN 978 0 7496 7500 4

A catalogue record for
this book is available
from the British Library.

Illustrator: Christopher O'Neill

The author, Jen Green, has written and edited many books
for young people on social issues and other topics.

Dewey Classification:
305.232

Our New Baby

Jen Green

Aladdin/Watts

London • Sydney

Contents

Introduction

These children are in the same class at school. One of their mums has just had a new baby. The other three have younger brothers and sisters. New babies bring changes to any family. In this book, they and other children talk about what a new brother or sister will mean to them.

I have a great time with my brother and sister.

To begin with, I wasn't sure about the new baby.

New babies are a lot of fun!

At first it can feel strange with a new baby at home.

Expecting A Baby

Dean and Amy are good friends at school. Dean has been looking forward to telling Amy his news. Dean's mum is pregnant – she will be having a new baby. The baby will be born in five months' time. Dean is excited about having a new baby brother or sister to play with. Is a new baby expected in your family?

You can have fun whether your family is big or small.

Do you want a new brother or a sister, Dean?

I don't mind – I'm looking forward to it either way.

▶ **Where Do Babies Come From?**

All babies begin from a tiny egg and a seed, called a sperm. The egg comes from the mother. The sperm comes from the father. When they join together, a new baby begins to grow inside the mother.

◀ **How Babies Grow**

A baby grows in the mother's womb, near the stomach. At first the new baby is tiny, but slowly it gets bigger. The mother's tummy gets larger, too. If your mum is pregnant you may be able to feel the baby moving in her tummy.

▶ **A Look Inside!**

Every few weeks a doctor or nurse will take a scan of a baby while it is growing inside your mum's womb. A scan allows the doctor to check on the baby's well-being. It can also show if your mum is expecting twins!

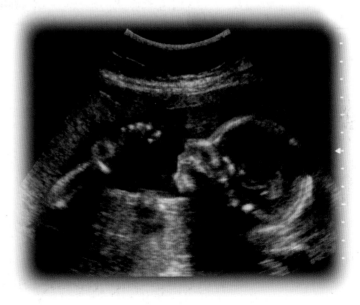

Dean, how do you feel about the new baby?
"I'm really excited. I've already got a younger sister, Sonia. I was only three when she was born so I don't remember much about it. This time I'm going to the clinic with mum for her check-up. There's a special machine there which shows you the shape of the baby on a TV screen, the scanner."

Mixed Feelings

Are you excited about having a new baby in your family?

I'm not sure. I might feel a bit left out.

You're going to have a little brother or sister.

You may feel happy…

…or you may feel unhappy.

Rosie lives with her mum and her stepdad, Steve. When Rosie went home with the news about Dean's family, Rosie's mum told her that she was also expecting a baby. Rosie says she has mixed feelings about it. If a new baby is expected in your family, how do you feel about it?

Story: What About Me?

1 A new baby was due in Hari's family. Hari was worried about it.

2 Hari's dad realised Hari was upset. He asked him what was wrong.

3 Hari's dad said that Hari had an important part to play in the family.

Why was Hari feeling worried?

If a new baby is due in your family, it's natural to feel a bit anxious. Like Hari, you may feel pleased, but also wonder quite how things will be. Hari talked to his dad. His dad explained they were so happy with Hari that they decided to have a new baby, too. If you feel worried, talk to your parents. Your mum and dad will understand how you feel.

Mixed Feelings

▶ Stepfamilies

If you live with only one of your parents, and your mum or dad is expecting a baby with a new partner, you might feel a bit left out. You might feel the new baby will get more love. But a new baby won't change your mum or dad's love for you. There will be enough love to go round for everyone.

Sorry, I'm too tired to play.

◀ Pleased Or Cross?

When a baby is expected, you may feel excited or proud. But you may also feel bored or impatient if your mum is feeling tired. You might also feel cross if she can't play with you as much as she did before.

▶ How Your Mum Feels

If your mum is expecting a baby, she may feel sick in the mornings. She may need more rest than usual. This is nothing to worry about. A growing baby uses up lots of your mum's energy. As the baby gets bigger, your mum may need help to lift heavy things.

Don't be sad about the new baby. It will all be OK.

▶ All Change

A baby means change for everyone. You may find this easy or you may find it hard, and wish that things could stay the way they were. If you already have a little brother or sister, he or she might feel upset about no longer being the youngest child.

◀ Getting Ready

There are many things to prepare for a new baby. The baby will need somewhere to sleep. You may have to move your things around, or move to a new room. Do you have any old toys which the new baby may like to play with?

▶ Boy Or Girl?

You may really want the new baby to be a boy or a girl – perhaps you would like a brother to play football with or a sister to go shopping with? But as your new brother or sister grows up, you will probably find that you enjoy playing with them either way!

Are you looking forward to the new baby, Rosie?

"Yes and no. My mum and dad don't live together any more. Now Mum and my stepdad, Steve, are having a new baby. I thought the new baby might be more special to them than me. But Mum says that having a new baby won't change the way she feels about me. I'm glad I spoke to her about it."

The Birth

It is Lucy's birthday tomorrow – she is going to be eleven. Her friend Mary has come around to play. Eleven years ago tomorrow Lucy was born in hospital. She thinks she was born at nine o' clock in the morning. Do you know what happened when you were born? Where did it happen and who was there?

It's often a rush before the birth.

I was born at home, but I don't remember it!

Of course you don't. You were only a baby!

14

The Birth

▶ In Hospital

After nine months in the mother's womb, the new baby is ready to be born. Your mum may go into hospital to have her baby. Your dad may go with her. While the baby is being born, your parents will ask a relative or a close friend to come and look after you.

◀ At Home

Your mum may decide to have her baby at home. A midwife, who is a special person who helps to deliver a baby, may come to help your mum. Your mum and dad may also arrange for a relative or friend to take care of you for a short while.

▶ How Long?

A baby's birth may take only a few hours. Or it can take most of a day. If your mum goes to hospital to have her baby, she may be home a few hours after it is born. Or she may stay in hospital for a few days. It's a big day when the baby comes home at last.

The Birth

Story: A New Brother

1 Fred's mum was having a baby in hospital. Fred's dad rang to speak to him.

2 The next day Fred went to see his mum in hospital. Fred's mum gave him a special hug.

3 Fred was excited when he saw the baby. His mum let Fred hold him for a while.

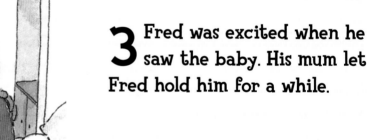

How did Fred feel about the birth of his baby brother?

Fred missed his mum when she was in hospital, even though his favourite aunt looked after him. When his dad rang to tell him about his new brother, Fred wasn't sure what he felt. But when he saw his mum, everything felt fine again. Don't worry if your mum goes away to have her baby. She and your dad will soon be home.

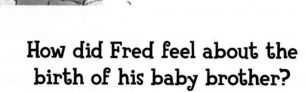

▶ Ready To Play?

You may want to play with your new brother or sister straight away. But newborn babies don't play much at first. They mostly sleep and feed. But they do like to be cuddled. Support the baby's head while you are cuddling him or her.

▼ Growing Up

Things change fast with a new baby. After three months the baby will be awake for longer, and will want you to play with him or her. Soon the baby will eat solid food. You might like to help with feeding – it may be messy!

The Birth

Lucy, do you know what happened when you were born?
"Yes, my mum told me. I was born in hospital. Mum said it took sixteen hours for me to be born. She said she was very pleased when I arrived at last! I've got two younger sisters. They were both born at home. My youngest sister, Jo, only took four hours to be born."

A Newborn Baby

Mark went to see his friend Sachin's new baby sister, Mina. Sachin said that at first he was a bit scared of holding Mina on his own. But he soon got used to it – now he feels very proud when he helps to look after her. Mina spends most of the time sleeping – Sachin can't wait until she's old enough to play games with him.

A baby feeds from the mum's breast.

Newborn babies are so small.

Mum says you must hold them firmly but carefully.

Or a baby feeds from a bottle.

▶ Playing With The Baby

Newborn babies are very small at first – but don't be scared to play with them! Babies like to look at people's faces. They learn to talk by copying the sounds we make, so sing nursery rhymes and talk to the baby. Make the baby laugh by being as silly as you like!

◀ Why Do Babies Cry?

Crying is a baby's only way of saying he or she needs something. A baby cries to get attention, if they are hungry or uncomfortable, or bored. Don't feel upset if the baby cries. You may get really good at knowing what the baby wants.

▶ Sleeping Problems

New babies need to feed often, including at night. Your mum and dad will be tired if they get up several times at night. You may also sleep badly, especially if you can hear the baby crying. There is nothing to worry about, so try to relax at night.

Story: Feeling Left Out

1 Ayisha and her family were very excited. The new baby had just come home.

2 But when friends came round, the baby was the centre of attention. Ayisha felt left out.

Isn't he lovely?

So sweet!

No one takes any notice of me.

3 Later Ayisha talked it over with her mum.

Why was Ayisha upset?

Ayisha was really pleased about the new baby. But she got upset when she felt no one was taking any notice of her any more. Things may feel different at first with a new baby at home. It will take time to get used to having a little stranger in the family. Talk things over with your mum and dad. Talking about your feelings nearly always helps.

▶ Good Times

You will probably have lots of different feelings about the baby. You may feel really pleased most of the time. You may love to play with the baby, and enjoy bath-times or feeds. You may be best at making the baby laugh.

◀ Looking After Baby

There are lots of simple ways you can help your mum and dad to look after a new baby. If you don't fancy changing a smelly nappy, don't worry! It can be fun helping at bathtime or pushing a pram through the park.

▼ Fed Up?

Sometimes you may feel bored or fed up about the baby. You may feel your mum and dad now have less time for you. Talk to your parents. Perhaps you can agree on a special time for you to spend time alone with your mum or dad.

Sachin, what was it like in your family when you were little?
"My older brother was eight and my sister was four when I was born. Mum said they helped a lot when I was little. They played with me and helped teach me to talk and to read. I learnt to walk quickly so I could keep up with them!"

A New Brother Or Sister

Jacob and Helena are showing each other pictures of the people in their families on Helena's computer. Jacob said he and his sister, Ruby, play together a lot. Helena said she used to get on badly with her younger sister, Sophie, but now they are good friends. If you've got brothers and sisters, how do you get on with them?

Some brothers and sisters get on. Others seem to fight a lot.

▶ Crawling And Talking

Of course, you can do hundreds of things a baby cannot do. Young babies cannot feed themselves or use a potty. But they grow up fast. At six months, a baby may start to crawl. At nine months, he or she may begin to say a few words.

◀ Safety First

Babies have no idea about what is safe. They put things into their mouths to taste them and to see if they are soft or hard. But you know what is not safe to eat, and places that aren't safe to go near. This can really help when you are keeping an eye on the baby.

▶ Younger Brothers And Sisters

If you have a younger brother or sister, he or she may not feel as you do about the baby. He or she is more likely to feel angry and a bit left out. If you spend time with your little brother or sister, it can really help them to feel special, too.

A New Brother Or Sister

Story: Feeling Jealous

1 Jack felt that his mum only ever played with his new sister. He felt angry and hit his mum.

2 Jack said his mum didn't care about him. Jack's mum said hitting wasn't allowed.

3 Next time he felt angry, Jack kicked a football. After a while he felt a bit better.

Why did Jack feel angry?

With the new baby, Jack felt cross and left out. Like him, you might feel angry. After all, you didn't choose to have a new baby in your family. You may feel like breaking something or even hitting someone. But this would only make things worse. Talk about your feelings. If you still feel like hitting out, hit something soft, like a cushion, or kick a football outside.

A New Brother Or Sister

▶ Family Fights

Sometimes you may quarrel with your brother or sister. But you probably stick up for each other when it matters most. Some brothers and sisters quarrel a lot when they are young, but become good friends later.

◀ Sharing

You may feel jealous of your brother or sister. You may find it hard to share your mum and dad. But just because your parents love your new sister or brother, it doesn't mean they will love you any less.

How do you get on with your sisters, Jacob?

"Ruby was born when I was three. I felt a bit jealous of her at first. Then, when I was six and Ruby was three, Jo was born. I liked playing with Jo, but I could see Ruby felt angry. I told Ruby I knew how she was feeling. Now Ruby and I play together lots."

Don't Forget...

1 How do you feel now about the new baby in your family, Rosie?

"At first I didn't like the idea of lots of change. After Mum and I talked about it, I felt better. I talked things over with Steve, my stepdad. I'm looking forward to it now. I'm going to help choose the baby's name."

2 Does a new baby make a big difference to a family, Dean?

"You may feel as if you get your own way less when there is a new baby around. But no one gets their own way all the time. Having a new baby in our family helped me to see that other people's feelings were important too. It's good, too, because we can have lots of fun now that our family is bigger."

3

Lucy, do you find it easy to talk things over in your family?

"When my sister Jill was small, for a bit I thought that Mum and Dad loved her more than me. But I told Mum and Dad how I felt. They said that they loved us both just as much, but sometimes Jill needed more looking after because she was a baby."

4

Do you like having a brother and sister, Sachin?

"Yeah. It's great. When I was small I learned from my big brother and sister. There's a video of my brother teaching me to walk. It's really funny. Now that I'm older, I'm looking forward to showing my little sister Mina how to do things."

Find Out More About New Babies

Helpful Addresses and Phone Numbers

Talking about problems or worries can really help. If you can't talk to someone close to you, then try ringing one of these organisations:

Childline
Tel: 0800 1111
A 24-hour free helpline for children. The number won't show up on a telephone bill if you ring them.

Kids Helpline, Australia
Tel: 1800 55 1800
A 24-hour free helpline for children. Also online help: www.kidshelp.com.au

NSPCC (National Society for the Prevention of Cruelty to Children)
Tel: 0808 800 500
Asian helpline: 0800 096 7719
A 24-hour free helpline offering counselling and practical advice for young people.

Parentline Plus
Tel: 0808 800 2222
A 24-hour free helpline offering counselling and support to parents on many issues, including helping your children to prepare for the arrival of a new baby.

On the Web

These websites are also helpful. You can get in touch with some of them using email:

www.kidshealth.org

www.nspcc.org.uk

www.childcarelink.org.uk

www.raisingkids.co.uk

www.parentlineplus.org.uk

www.kidshelp.com.au

www.parentlink.act.gov.au

Further Reading

If you want to read more about having a new baby in the family, try:

Talking About Stepfamilies by Sarah Levete (Aladdin/Watts)

How Did I Begin? by Mick Manning (Franklin Watts)

Baby On The Way by William and Martha Sears (Little Brown)

A New Baby Is Coming by Emily Menendez-Aponte (Elf-Help Books)

There's a Brand New Baby at Our House… and I'm the Big Sister! by Susan Russell Ligon (Tommy Nelson)

Let's Talk About: Where Babies Come From by Robie H. Harris (Walker Books)

Index

Photocredits

All photos from istockphoto.com.

All the photos in this book have been posed by models.